Sports

I Can Go Fishing

By Edana Eckart

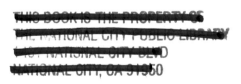
Children's Press®
A Division of Scholastic Inc.
New York / Toronto / London / Auckland / Sydney
Mexico City / New Delhi / Hong Kong
Danbury, Connecticut

Photo Credits: Cover and all photos by Maura B. McConnell
Contributing Editor: Jennifer Silate
Book Design: Mindy Liu

Library of Congress Cataloging-in-Publication Data

Eckart, Edana.
  I can go fishing / by Edana Eckart.
  p. cm. — (Sports)
  Summary: A young girl goes out in a boat with her father and learns to fish.
  ISBN 0-516-24279-2 (lib. bdg.) — ISBN 0-516-24371-3 (pbk.)
  1. Fishing—Juvenile literature. [1. Fishing.] I. Title.

SH445 .E25 2003
799.1—dc21

                                                    2002009376

Contents

My name is Julie.

My dad and I are going **fishing**.

This is my **fishing rod**.

I will use it to catch fish.

We get into our boat.

I put on my **life jacket**.

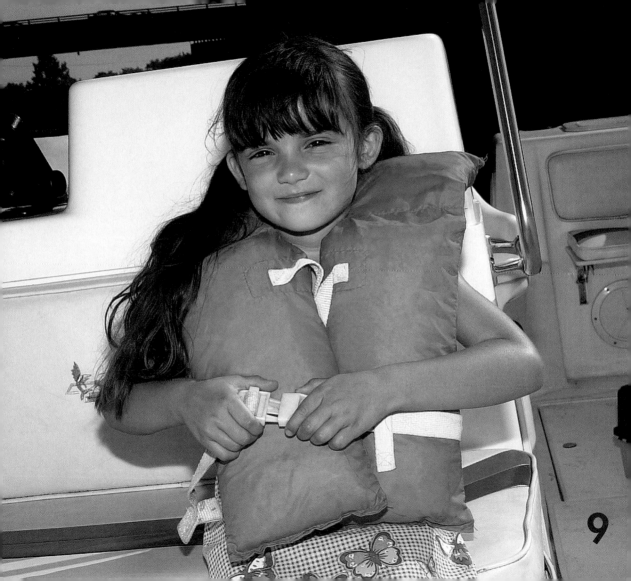

9

Dad drives the boat out onto the water.

I like riding in our boat.

11

It is time to fish.

Dad ties a **hook** onto my **fishing line**.

He is very **careful**.

13

Dad helps me **cast** my hook out into the water.

It goes far!

15

I feel something pull
on my line.

It is a fish!

I turn the **reel** to pull
in the fish.

16

17

Look, I caught a fish!

It is big.

18

19

Fishing is fun.

I want to go fishing again soon.

New Words

careful (**kair**-fuhl) paying close attention

cast (**kast**) to throw a fishing line or net
into the water

fishing (**fish**-ing) to try to catch a fish

fishing line (**fish**-ing **line**) a thin string that is used
with a rod, hook, and reel to catch a fish

fishing rod (**fish**-ing **rod**) a long, flexible pole used
with a hook, line, and reel to catch fish

hook (**huk**) a curved piece of metal with a sharp
point at one end that is used to catch fish

life jacket (**life jak**-it) a jacket that will keep you
afloat if you fall into the water

reel (**reel**) a spool on which the fishing line is wound

To Find Out More

Books

Fishing in a Brook: Angling Activities for Kids
by G. Lawson Drinkard, III
Gibbs Smith Publisher

Fishing with Foster
by Turner Bowman
Always Kids Publishing

Web Site
Kids' Fishing Corner
http://www.fishing-hunting.com/kidsfishing/
Play games, learn about fishing, and do much more on this Web site.

Index

About the Author
Edana Eckart has written several children's books. She enjoys bike riding with her family.

Reading Consultants
Kris Flynn, Coordinator, Small School District Literacy, The San Diego County Office of Education

Shelly Forys, Certified Reading Recovery Specialist, W.J. Zahnow Elementary School, Waterloo, IL

Sue McAdams, Former President of the North Texas Reading Council of the IRA, and Early Literacy Consultant, Dallas, TX